Pensamentos

Bits of Wisdom from

Rubem Alves

Other New London Librarium

Titles by Rubem Alves

The Best Chronicles of Rubem Alves

Tender Returns

Art of Love

Concerto for Body and Soul

Pensamentos

Bits of Wisdom from
Rubem Alves

Translated by
Glenn Alan Cheney

New London Librarium

Pensamentos: Bits of Wisdom from Rubem Alves
by Rubem Alves
Translated and edited by Glenn Alan Cheney

Copyright © 2019 Glenn Alan Cheney

Published by
New London Librarium
Hanover, CT 06350
NLLibrarium.com

All rights reserved. No part of this book may be reproduced in any medium whatsoever without the express permission of the translator or publisher.

ISBNs
Hardcover: 978-1-947074-37-8
Paperback:978-1-947074-36-1
eBook: 978-1-947074-38-5

Printed in the United States

The brief thoughts in this book were excerpted from the following books, all published by Editora Papirus.

As Melhores Crônicas de Rubem Alves

O Retorno e Terno

O Amor Que Acende a Lua

Sobre o Tempo e a Eternidade

Concerto para Corpo e Alma

Contents

Foreword : *ix*

First Persons : 13

Souls and Invisibilities : 25

Wisdom, Wonders, Words : 45

Bodies, Pains, Pleasures : 71

Love, Longings, and Other Callings : 93

Questionable Intentions : 137

The Ends : 155

Acknowledgements : 175

About Rubem Alves : 176

About the Translator : 177

New London Librarium : 178

Foreword

You could read this book in under an hour.

But then you will not have read it. You will have missed it as if in a car that zipped by reflections in a pond, a fawn at the edge of woods, a hitch-hiker with tales to tell. You will have swallowed the words without tasting the ideas—a Thanksgiving feast gulped down as if no more than a compacted pill of nutrient extract. You will have missed the depths of the vast blank spaces between Rubem Alves's succinct and subtle pronouncements.

Those spaces are indeed blank. Empty. The words that appear among them are excerpts from more densely populated fields, the contexts of tales, arguments, explanations, reminders, analyses, and assorted wonderings. Here the contexts have been peeled away, leaving the stark-naked nuggets of ideas, seeds deprived of pods.

The open space around each isolated idea is new world for the reader to explore. It's a place to wander at whim, at leisure, at will. It's what Rubem would want you to do—take your time, be a child for a while, think the unthought, noddle your way through oddities and contradictions until you find the truths that render them intelligible. Look for the sonata in a sunset, the prayers in poetry, the communion of sadness shared, the whiff of uncertainty in love.

Though a very productive man—a theologian, psychoanalyst, philosopher, professor, and author of hundreds of essays and more than forty books—Rubem Alves was an advocate of idleness. He wrote of the importance of wasting time, putting things off, doting on the banal, simply doing nothing. But he also kept books in the bathroom so he could do two things at once.

He would want you to read this book slowly—to give good thought to the sparse sentences on a given page, then waste a little time wandering around the blank space. He would want his idea to blossom into your idea, a seed nurtured into a flower. "To germinate," he writes herein, "a seed needs a hole in the earth to take it in....The germination of listening...requires time and silence."

He would also want you to read the complete essays, found in other books, the full context of the brief statements transplanted here. But your mind won't wander through its own thought-fields if it has already been captured by his explanations. Ideas are wonderful things, but as he explains, once an idea is expressed, it becomes an enchanted bird trapped in a cage of words. He writes a lot about birds in cages and birds flying free. He was a big advocate of the latter. Advocate? No. He worshipped birds left free to fly, birds beyond the reach of science, words, and the strictures of reason.

I daresay Rubem Alves would be honored to have this book find its way to your bathroom, the most exclusive and exalted of libraries. It's a good place to read a little and think a lot. Savor each page. Savor the space. Give your imagination time to wander in search of meaning and understanding. Don't let the book or the bathroom be cages. Let them be as wide as the sky and as deep as a soul. Read slowly. Think big. Fly free.

GLENN ALAN CHENEY
HANOVER, CONN.

First Persons

I have learned

that the best way to chase away the ridiculous

is to be the first to laugh at it.

Yes, I want to live many more years.

But not at any price.

I want to be alive as long as my capacity

to be moved by beauty is alive.

I want to be cremated because I don't like closed spaces.

Ashes can be released to the wind

or laid like fertilizer at the roots of a tree.

Thus I can become flower or cloud.

Speleology is the science of caverns. I studied a speleology dedicated to exploring the caverns of the soul. The soul is a maze of caverns lit by a light that infiltrates through narrow cracks, caverns that grow ever deeper and darker. Outside is the sunlit world, "a great fair, all tents and street performers" (Fernando Pessoa), a lot of people, yackety-yack, shouting, gossip, laughter, everybody talking, nobody listening, everybody exchanging words they know, and everybody wearing smiling masks. The entrance to the cavern is hidden by vegetation. Few find it. Few have the courage to enter. Inside, everything is different. The spaces shaped by the millennia call for few words. Voices turn into whispers. But eyes grow. And so we go descending, deeper and deeper, until we find ourselves. There is solitude and silence. The truth of the soul is beyond words. It cannot be spoken.

I am a mystic.

Contrary to religious mystics,

who close their eyes

to see God, the Virgin, and the angels,

I open my eyes wide

to see the fruits and vegetables in the stands at the market.

Each fruit is a wonder, a miracle.

An onion is a miracle.

I am a builder of altars.

I build altars on the edge of a dark and silent abyss.

I build them with poetry and music.

The fires I light within them

illuminate my face and warm it.

But the abyss remains dark and silent.

I am horrified by our impotence
before the destructive power of companies
that raze nature out of love of money.
But I am more horrified to think
that people are not horrified.

To the infernal Descartes, with his

"I think, therefore I am,"

I say:

"I am possessed by music, therefore I am."

Time is an empty cup

that can be filled with life.

⁓❋⁓

Time can be measured

by the ticks of a clock,

or by the beats of a heart.

Soul and Invisibilities

The truth of the soul is beyond words.

It cannot be spoken.

The soul, at its deepest place, is a scene of happiness.

To live is to go out

either seeking a happy scene or trying to build one.

The love of a man or a woman

happens when all of a sudden,

when you see a face,

you have the impression that you've seen it there

in that happy scene of the soul.

All Gods

are portraits

of those

who believe in them.

The soul is a butterfly.
There comes a moment when a voice tells us
that the time has come for metamorphosis.

Suffering prepares the soul
for a vision of something new.

The soul wishes to rise.

It wants to leave its corporeal prison

and return to the luminescent world it came from.

But the body that is its prison is made of other stuff.

It's material.

It, too, wishes to return to its world. It wants to descend.

The soul is lightness. The body is weight.

There's a conflict.

But it doesn't happen within the soul,

which is an arrow shot at infinity.

The soul itself has just one desire.

It craves the noble things above:

truth, beauty, and the good.

Real safety exists only inside a cage.

Inside cages, there is no joy.

Butterflies live shut up in cocoons for only a while.

Suddenly they go out into life,

into flight,

into danger,

into joy.

Who are we? We are creatures born for the theater.

We are, essentially, actors. We play roles all the time.

The soul is the script of a play.

To know the soul, all you have to do is get up on a stage,

distribute masks and parts, and let the show begin.

As the show unfolds, the soul reveals itself.

What does it reveal?

Your face without a mask?

No.

It reveals the masks and roles that you prefer.

We may not believe in gods,
but we'd do well to wish they existed.

The wings of the soul are called courage.

Courage is not the absence of fear.

It is going forth despite fear.

Realism confirms the created.

Surrealism recreates the created.

God gave us the wings of thought.

Men gave us the cages of religion.

The path to truth requires forgetting.

It is necessary to forget what's been learned

in order to remember that which knowledge has buried.

Everything that lives is a pulse of the holy.

The birds in the skies,

the lilies of the field,

even the most insignificant grasshopper,

with it rhythmic *crick-crick-crick*,

are songs of the Great Mystery.

The popcorn kernel isn't all it ought to be.

It ought to be that which comes after the pop.

The kernel is us:

hard tooth-breakers inappropriate for consumption.

By the power of fire we can, all of a sudden,

transform ourselves into something else.

I see religious people close their eyes when they pray.

They believe that, to see God, one must not see the world.

They do not know that the beauty of nature is the mirror

where God contemplates himself.

The soul is larger than the astronomic universe.

Psychoanalysis is a travel guide.

※

Every soul is a song being played.

Life is not a biological thing.

Life is an aesthetic entity.

Hope is a hallucinogen.

Wisdom, Wonder, Words

The Church found the unconscious through sin.

Psychoanalysis found it through neurosis and psychosis.

But there's another way: that of poets.

Poets found the unconscious through Beauty.

For them, the center of the unconscious is a garden.

"In the old days" is a time that has gone

yet refuses to go away.

It remains inside us,

tormenting the heart with longing.

Pure intellect hates repetition.

It's always after something new.

Once in possession of certain knowledge,

it doesn't keeping going over it again and again.

It says, "Got it," and moves on to something different.

Often, in literature, the short is larger than the long.

There are poems that contain a universe.

Science is knowledge of the world.

Wisdom is knowledge of life.

Words are cages.

That which is spoken is that which has been caged.

A god who can be caged by words is not God.

God is an enchanted bird. For him there are no words.

But men insist on caging him.

Don't get upset about what has not happened

and might not ever happen.

Take care of what happens tomorrow

tomorrow.

Words have meaning only when

they help us see the world better.

We learn words to improve our vision.

Cowboys use lassos of leather

to catch cows that got loose.

Psychoanalysts use lassos of words

to catch ideas that got loose.

Intelligent people, who go through life
thinking and having different ideas,
are dangerous.
The socio-political order is better served by people who
always think the same thoughts—that is,
dumbed-down people.

There is only one way to exorcize the demon of death:

to speak about it honestly, to call it by its name.

Words are powerful things.

They have the power of infinite error.

Many a sonorous word

serves to disguise ignorance.

Wisdom is the art of savoring life

the way one savors food.

You should speak only

when your speech improves on silence.

If your talk doesn't improve on silence,

it is preferable that you remain silent

so that silence can be heard.

Being dumb is just this: to think the same thoughts—

even if they are grandiose thoughts.

Proof of that is in the societies of bees and ants,

notable for their stability and capacity to survive.

Mothers are the place where

you can cry without being embarrassed.

Wonder resides in that which is dreamt.

Real facts are only good for tying up fantasies,

like a nail holding up a painting.

Nobody sees the nails.

We don't see what we see.

We see what we are.

Those who see beauty in the world

are those who have beauty inside.

A curious tendency in human beings:
They believe everything that is repeated by others,
even when it's asinine.

Words that teach are cages

for birds that can be caged.

Experts, all of them,

are caged birds.

Wisdom lives within us.

People don't think.

Individuals think.

Thinking is a dangerous thing...

A book is a toy made of letters.

To read is to play.

Bodies, Pleasures, Pain

Worlds reside in the guts of men.

A wake is a magic ritual in which

the guts of the dead are contemplated.

To do so, there is no need to open the body.

Throughout a life, bodies let guts be seen

by means of the mouth.

Our guts aren't viscera.

They are words.

We are the things that reside inside us.

That's why some people are lovely not for their faces

but for the exuberance of their inner world.

Candles cry as they shine.

Their tears, born of fire,

spill over and run down their body.

They cry because they know that,

to shine, they must die.

The ear is feminine,

an emptiness that waits and welcomes,

that allows itself to be penetrated.

Speech is masculine,

something that grows and penetrates

the empty places in the soul.

There is no art without sadness.

The beauty of art counterbalances the sadness of life.

What can be taught are things

that reside in the outside world:

astronomy, physics, chemistry grammar,

anatomy, numbers, letters, words.

But there are things that are not on the outside...

things that reside inside the body. They are buried in the

flesh as if they were seeds in waiting...

Sunset is beautiful because its colors are ephemeral
and in a few minutes it will cease to be.
The sonata is beautiful because its life is short.

The precision of numbers measures the time

of money and machines.

Love's time is measured with the body.

Beauty does not do away with tragedy,

but it makes it tolerable.

The dream of every man is to have his penis

under the control of reason.

But the penis ignores reason.

It has its own ideas.

You never know what ideas it will have.

Our bodies are dreams incarnate.

Mental health—

that condition in which ideas behave themselves,

always balanced, foreseeable, without surprises,

obedient to the commands of duty,

everything in its place like soldiers in rank order,

never allowing the body to miss work

or do something unexpected.

Sexual desire in the adolescent

is independent of any object.

It is pure, crude, irrational desire.

Things that can be taught

are things that can be spoken.

Which is more important:

To know answers

or to know which questions to ask?

It's always children who ask the best questions.

A sea comprehended

is no more

than an aquarium.

Happiness is an experience of fitting together,

quite like the fitting together of the bodies of people

in love, in the act of love.

In each of us resides an Emptiness

that awaits something to fill it.

We are all feminine.

A baby knows nothing.

The world is reduced to a singular magical object:

the breast of the mother.

There is born the primal philosophy,

the one that summarizes all the others:

the world is here to be eaten.

Beauty has an inebriating effect.

When the soul is touched by beauty,

the brain doesn't ask questions.

We are many things. And that's where the problem lies.

The body is the residence of many:

angels and demons, witches and fairies,

lovers and executioners, vegetarians and carnivores,

buffoons and undertakers, philosophers and drunks.

They all reside in the same body.

The body is a hostel.

Love, Longings, and Other Callings

In a vocation, a person finds happiness in the act itself.

In a profession, pleasure is found not in the act

but in the gain derived.

Speech is masculine.

Fullness, semen, seed, penetration, ejaculation.

According to the *Aurélio* dictionary, that word, *ejaculate*,

normally used for a jet of sperm,

also means "to utter, to say out loud."

Ejaculating sperm and speaking are the same thing.

Prayer is longing

transformed into poetry.

———

Prayers and poems are the same thing:

words pronounced in silence,

asking that silence speak to us.

We are lovers before we ever meet the man or woman who

will be the object of our love.

We are like the baby who loves the breast

even before first finding it.

How can one long for someone who is present?

The answer is simple:

We long for a person who is present

when he or she is in the process of leaving.

We don't love people who talk pretty.

We love people who listen pretty.

Those who drink together

at the same fountain of sadness

discover, to their surprise,

that shared sadness

turns into communion.

To be at ease like trees and animals,

we will need to have no heart.

We are condemned to suffering

because we are condemned to love.

Jealousy is the painful awareness

that love's object is not property.

It can fly away at any moment.

That's why love is painful—

it's the whiff of uncertainty.

Love letters aren't written to give news,

not to say anything,

but so that separated hands

can touch the same sheet of paper.

Vocation is an inner call of love—

not love for a man or woman

but for a *thing-to-be-done*.

This *thing-to-be-done* marks the place

where those who are called

want to make love with the world.

Listening is feminine.

The erect penis is a poverty.

It's a beseeching, a prayer for a vagina to take it in.

To germinate, a seed needs a hole in the earth to take it in.

Speech is poor, a lacking. It seeks the emptiness of the ear.

The ejaculation of speech, being masculine,

happens in a moment.

But the germination of listening, being feminine,

requires time and silence.

The vocation of poets: to put words in places where the pain is too bad. Not to end it but so it can turn into something eternal: a star in the firmament, shining sans surcease in the dark night.

The ethical ideal in politics can never be reached.

Only the weak invoke ethical arguments,

because those are the only weapons they bear.

To love is to have a bird on your finger.

When you have a bird on your finger,

you know that at any moment,

it can fly away.

Love prefers the light of candles.

Maybe because that's everything we wish for a beloved—

that she or he be a soft light

that helps us tolerate the terror of the night.

Many married couples never separate
because they can't stand the idea of
the other in freedom and happiness.

The sadness of love is emptiness desiring fullness.

Socrates said that Eros was born

from the marriage of Poverty and Plentitude.

Love is a hole in the soul. One who loves is poor.

He or she lacks something–

a puzzle piece fitting into another piece.

The feeling of love is a longing for the piece you lack.

What lover could tolerate a kiss that never ended?

A love letter is a paper that connects two lonelinesses.

It is necessary to choose.

Because time flies.

There's no time for everything.

It is necessary to learn the art of letting go

so we can dedicate ourselves to the essential.

Longing is like hunger.

Hunger, too, is an emptiness.

The body knows when something is lacking.

Hunger is the longing of the body.

Longing is the hunger of the soul.

Solidarity is neither taught nor ordered nor produced.

Solidarity has to sprout and grow like a seed.

Love has no why.

It loves because it loves.

Teaching is an exercise in immortality.

In a certain way we go on living in those whose eyes learn

to see the world through the wizardry of our words.

Thus the teacher never dies.

This is what we love in others—

the empty place they open

where our fantasies can grow.

Nature is a good psychoanalyst,

charging nothing for

the dreams of love she makes us dream.

Does the future exist? It may.

I don't know how things will be,

but through fantasy it become the present.

That is exactly what gives rise to hope.

Isn't that what love is?—

a desire to eat, a desire to be eaten?

God is our heart's suspicion

that the universe pulses

with a heart like ours.

Longing is the pocket

where the soul keeps

that which it has tasted and approved.

Longing is the face of eternity

reflected in the river of time.

Schools exist not to teach the answers

but to teach the questions.

The answers allow us to walk on terra firma.

The questions allow us to enter the unknown sea.

The objective of education is

to increase the possibilities of pleasure and joy.

Poets are religious people
who don't need religion.
The wonders of the world suffice.

We lose ourselves in multiplicity.

We do not know our desires...

... The heart that pursues the many

is a fragmented heart that does not rest.

People who think in minutes

don't have the patience to plant trees.

※

Planting a tree

says No to the desert.

Love cannot abide without response.

We are what we love.

Don't fight with your illness.

It has come to stay.

Try to understand what it wants to teach you.

It wants you to be wise.

It wants to resuscitate your dormant feelings.

It wants to give you the sensibility of artists.

For poets,

the world is a mirror of a thousand sides

for the soul to contemplate itself.

The professor who is contracted

to give lessons in his or her discipline,

and only gives lessons in that discipline,

the professor who doesn't dream the big dream,

who's just an employee,

that one is a stone in a shoe.

Cooks who don't take seriously
the pleasure in the food they serve
soon lose employment.
Unfortunately, the same is not true
of professors and philosophers.

Knowledge alone doesn't make anyone desire

to plant a tree and hang a child's swing.

For that, you need love.

Worlds that are to be created,

before they exist as reality,

exist as fantasies of love.

Among all the vocations,

politics is the most noble.

Among all the professions,

politics is the most vile.

Questionable Intentions

Today there is no reason for optimism.

Only hope is possible.

Hope is the opposite of optimism...

...Optimism is happiness "because of":

It's a human and natural thing.

Hope is happiness "in spite of":

It's a divine thing.

Optimism has its roots in time.

Hope has its roots in eternity.

Wherever man goes, there you find signs

of his call to destruction and devastation.

They don't go to the beach

to hear the music of the sea.

They go to the beach

to socialize their insanity and agitation.

They don't go to the woods and waterfalls

to recuperate their lost harmony with nature.

They go to woods and waterfalls

to leave their trash and excrement.

What makes the world human isn't things.

It's relationships.

※

Societies are built when men agree on big things.

Friendships happen when men agree on small things.

Science—poor little thing!

So certain, so full of research and truths.

It knows how to send a man to the moon,

but it doesn't know how to make a person love.

Crime doesn't start with
the finger that pulls the trigger.
It starts with the one
who makes the gun.

The young are birds that take off in the morning.

Their flights are arrows in all directions.

Their eyes are fascinated by ten thousand things.

Their world is the world of multiplicity.

With adults, the opposite happens.

For them, multiplicity is a spell that imprisons,

a trap they fall into.

They hate multiplicity,

but they don't know how to free themselves.

Priests, pastors, and psychoanalysts are dangerous.

They belong to the same class:

men who are alone with needy women.

If we asked a Hebrew prophet

"What is politics?"

he would respond,

"The art of gardening applied to public things."

The forests were cut by

businessmen, developers, lovers of profit short on vision.

[To them], a tree standing up isn't worth anything.

A tree on the ground is worth money.

Each day we are new.

But memory of what we were yesterday

ruins the newness of being.

Our brains are more and more connected

to videos and computers,

less and less nature.

There are children who have never seen a real hen,

never smelled a pine,

never heard the song of a goldfinch,

and have no pleasure in playing with dirt.

They think dirty is dirty.

They don't know dirt is life.

The conscious ego knits sweaters of words

and gives them the name *Truth*.

The body weaves carpets of words

and gives them the name *Beauty*.

Power's rationale
transforms crimes into heroism.

Reason has nothing to do with happiness.

Reason is like those genies who come out from a lamp.

They don't have a will of their own,

nor do they have imagination.

All they have is power.

Thoughts are the wings that God gave us.

So everything that prohibits the free flight of thought

is contrary to our destiny.

The issue isn't thinking right or thinking wrong.

Ultimately, who knows what's right and wrong?

What would you tell someone who goes through life spreading feces wherever he goes? They do that and then complain that life stinks. With good reason. The number of people unhappy because of the stink of their own feces is much greater than you think. So be careful when you whine about life. Gripes about life often reveal the intestinal disturbances of those who do the griping.

The Ends

Abysms always tell the truth.

Everything that is perfect asks to die.

After death, the poem becomes silence—emptiness.

Then something else is born in its place: longing.

Longing only flourishes in absence.

Mankind lost Paradise

when we left off being children who play

and became adults who work.

Schools exist to turn children who play

into adults who work.

People who know the existing solutions

are perpetual beggars.

People who learn to invent new solutions

are those who open doors previously closed.

The issue isn't knowing the existing solutions,

it's learning new ways to survive.

Forgetting is often a gift.

It is much more difficult than remembering.

I know my words are useless.

Death makes everything useless.

When pain dies down,

it's because forgetfulness

has done its job.

Wisdom begins when we learn to tell time.

When you watch time,

you know that time does not add up.

It only subtracts down.

There's a death that happens before death.

It's when one concludes that there is no reason to live.

When there is no reason to live,

in come the reasons to die.

To be beautiful, life should be surrounded by

truth, goodness, and freedom.

These are things worth dying for.

We remain human as long as there exists within us

the hope of beauty and joy.

One the possibility of feeling joy

or enjoying beauty

has died,

our body transforms

into the husk of an empty cicada.

The rich don't save leftovers.

They don't need to. It's humiliating.

The leftovers of the rich go into the trash.

The leftovers of the poor go into the soup pot.

The most rudimentary soups are made from

leftovers destined for the trash.

Soup is a magical potion through which

that which was lost is saved from perdition

and redirected into the cycle of life and pleasure.

How ironic that life only happens across time,

yet the whole of life is a struggle

to keep time from passing.

We can be free of stress

only when we understand

that it's a symptom of

death's dominion over life.

Sunsets are a poetic metaphor.

If we feel that, it's because it sad beauty

lives inside our own bodies.

We are crepuscular beings.

Tiredness is the time to go.

Leave-taking is sad, but it's what must be.

Life is made of good-byes.

For them, tears are sweet.

They run like water that blossoms

from a gentle spring.

The newborn in the tight, dark canal
is totally alone and abandoned.
One who is dying is also
absolutely alone and abandoned.
Those who love and surround the dying
are far away, very far away.
The hands they extend
do not reach across the abyss.
Death is always a sinking into abandonment.

It's eternity that gives meaning to life.

Eternity isn't time without end.

Time without end is intolerable.

Have you ever imagined a song without end,

a kiss without end,

a book without end?

All that is beautiful must end.

All that is beautiful must die.

Acknowledgements

New London Librarium would like to thank Senior Editor Denise Dembinski for scrutinizing every word of this book. We also extend our gratitude to Raquel Alves, the Instituto Rubem Alves, and Editora Papirus for allowing us to bring a few of the thoughts of Rubem Alves to the English-speaking world.

About Rubem Alves

Rubem Alves (1933–2014) was a theologian, philosopher, educator, psychoanalyst, and one of Brazil's most popular writers. Born in Boa Esperança, Minas Gerais, he went on to earn a Ph.D. from Princeton Theological Seminary. He also trained and practiced as a psychoanalyst. His most recent professorship was at the Universidade Estadual at Campinas. He is the author of hundreds of essays and 40 books on pedagogy, theology, philosophy, and life in general. His works have been published in 13 countries and translated into various languages. More information is available at the Instituto Rubem Alves in Campinas, São Paulo State, Brazil (www.rubemalves.com.br).

About the Translator

Glenn Alan Cheney is a translator, writer, and editor in Hanover, Conn. His more than 25 books explore myriad topics, including Brazil's Estrada Real and the Quilombo dos Palmares, nuns, Chernobyl, nuclear issues, the Pilgrims, Abraham Lincoln, Mahatma Gandhi, Central American insurrections, Amazonia, bees, cats, death and burial, the end of the world, incarceration, and Swaziland, as well as novels, stories, poems, and essays. He is the founder and managing editor of New London Librarium.

New London Librarium

New London Librarium is a small literary press in Hanover, Conn. that specializes in works that deserve publication but whose market would not justify publication by a larger house. Special series include art, Brazil, Catholic issues, controversial issues, fiction, and history. Many of its titles are translations of Brazilian classics. For more information and the catalog, see NLLibrarium.com.

Made in the USA
Columbia, SC
26 April 2020

94196021R00107